~THE~ WHALERS

Peter Chrisp

Dangerous Waters

MONSTERS OF THE DEEP
PIRATES AND TREASURE
VOYAGES OF EXPLORATION
THE WHALERS

Fearsome Creatures

BIRDS OF PREY
LAND PREDATORS
NIGHT CREATURES
WHEN DINOSAURS RULED THE
EARTH

Frontiers

JOURNEYS INTO THE UNKNOWN
MAPS AND GLOBES
THE WILD, WILD WEST
THE WORLD'S WILD PLACES

The Earth's Secrets

FOSSILS AND BONES
THE HIDDEN PAST
THE SEARCH FOR RICHES
VOLCANO, EARTHQUAKE AND
FLOOD

Produced by
Roger Coote Publishing, 68 Florence Road
Brighton, East Sussex BN1 6DJ, England

Series designer: Jane Hannath
Book designer: David Armitage

First published in 1995 by
Wayland (Publishers) Limited, 61 Western Road
Hove, East Sussex BN3 1JD, England

© Copyright 1995 Wayland (Publishers) Limited

British Library Cataloguing in Publication Data

Chrisp, Peter
    The Whalers. - (Quest Series)
    I. Title II. Series
    639.28

    ISBN 0 7502 1201 2

Printed and bound in Italy by
G. Canale & C.S.p.A., Turin

Picture acknowledgements
B & C Alexander 17b, 38b/David Rootes, 40c/Ian
Cumming, 40tr/Ian Cumming, 44b; Bruce Coleman
16r/Fred Bruemmer, 34t, 38t/Dr Eckart Pott, 39/Ken
Balcomb, 45c/Jeff Foott Productions, 45b/Johnny Johnson;
Environmental Picture Library 44c/Steve Morgan; ET
Archive 4b; Mary Evans Picture Library 4l, 9t, 9c, 14, 24b,
26t, 29b, 31r, 36, 37t, 37b; Fotomas Index title page, 9b,
23r, 24l, 24b; The Kendall Whaling Museum, Sharon,
Massachusetts, USA 22-23; Kobal Collection 31t/Warner
Bros; Frank Lane Picture Agency 7t/Steve McCutcheon;
Greenpeace 42/Weyler, 44tr; Peter Newark's Historical
Pictures 6, 11l, 15, 19t, 20, 21t, 21b, 22t, 30, 33b; Old
Dartmouth Historical Society - New Bedford Whaling
Museum 12t, 12b, 17t, 18t, 18b, 19b, 28, 32, 33t; Ann
Ronan/Image Select 13, 25, 29; Zefa 5/B Talbot, 7b/Steve
McCutcheon, 8/Steve McCutcheon, 38l/Abril, 43/Pacific
Stock, Jim Watt. The artwork is by Peter Bull 5, 13, 41;
Barbara Loftus 4, 16l; David McAllister 10-11, 11tr, 27b,
35.

CONTENTS

WHO WERE THE FIRST WHALERS?

THE icy waters of the Arctic are home to a strange-looking animal with an enormous mouth, like an arched doorway. It is called the bowhead whale. Like you and me, the bowhead is a warm-blooded mammal. It is able to live in the freezing water only because it is wrapped in a 50-cm thick layer of fat called blubber.

The bowhead's huge mouth is lined with 4-m long strips of a springy substance, called baleen. The whale uses these to trap krill - tiny shrimp-like creatures that are its food.

The Inuit whale hunt

The first whale hunters were native people of the far north, called the Inuit. Each spring, as the sea ice melts, bowhead whales swim north from their winter home in the Bering Sea; and each spring, for thousands of years, the Inuit have waited for them.

The Inuit believed that the bowhead allowed itself to be killed, and that after death its spirit went to live in another bowhead, which would come back to offer itself the following year. But the whale would only do this if they treated it with respect. The Inuit thought that the whale, out at sea, knew about the preparations that were being made for its hunt. It was easily offended if things were not done properly.

The Inuit hunted bowheads in big boats called umiaks. The one-man boats, kayaks, were used to hunt smaller animals such as seals.

Why whales can be hunted

Although whales live in the sea, they breathe air. They need to come up to the surface regularly to get rid of stale, used air and take in fresh air. When the whale blows out, its warm breath meets the cooler air and forms a spray of mist. This is called the whale's spout, and it can often be seen from a long distance.

Whales behave in a predictable way. They regularly move from one part of the ocean to another - from feeding places to breeding places, from summer to winter homes. The early whalers noticed this and they learned when and where to watch for the whales.

Main picture This is the sight that every whaler waits for - the spout, or spray of mist, showing the presence of a whale at the surface.

Inset The map shows the regular movement of the bowhead whales, which brings them to the land of the Inuit every year in spring.

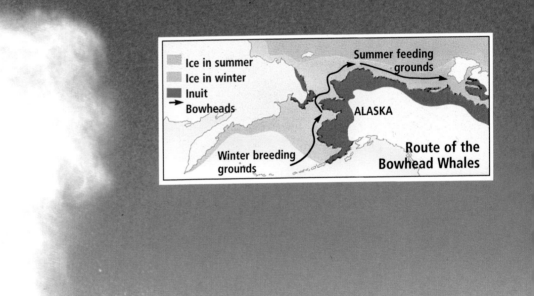

Ice in summer
Ice in winter
Inuit
Bowheads

ALASKA

Summer feeding grounds

Winter breeding grounds

Route of the Bowhead Whales

In March, the women sewed new clothes for their husbands and a new skin cover for the umiak, the whaling boat. Anything old or dirty would upset the whales. Meanwhile, the men sat together quietly, thinking about whales.

Singing the whales ashore

An important part of whaling was the singing of songs that were believed to have magical powers. There were different songs for different purposes - to bring good weather, to attract the whales and to make the harpoons stick. The men also wore magic whaling charms, such as bone carved into the shape of whales and strands of hair from the heads of famous dead whalers.

When everything was ready, the men set off for their whaling camp on the ice, dragging their umiak along with them. Here they sat and waited for the bowheads to arrive.

A whaler with a heavy harpoon fixed to an animal skin float. This hunter belongs to the Nootka people, who live to the south of the Inuit.

When a bowhead was seen, the men set off, paddling their umiak. Approaching the whale, they hurled their stone-headed harpoons with all their strength. These were attached to inflated seal skins, which acted as a drag on the whale, forcing it to surface. When the wounded bowhead became tired, the men came in close for the kill - stabbing it again and again. This was the most dangerous moment: if the whale overturned the boat, the men had little chance of surviving in the icy water.

Today, the Inuit still hunt bowhead whales. Here, a group of hunters waits on the ice beside their umiak boat, just as they have done for thousands of years.

A dead bowhead is dragged to the shore, where it is stripped of its blubber.

Welcoming the whale

All the villagers helped to drag the dead whale ashore. Then the wife of the chief whaler greeted the whale. She poured water over its huge mouth, saying, 'It is good that you are come to us.' Her husband added, 'Here is water; you will want to drink. Next spring come back to our boat.'

Using the whale

North Alaska is one of the coldest and harshest places on earth. Lacking trees and plants, the Inuit hunters there depended for many things on the whales they killed. The skin, fins, blubber, flesh, tongue, intestines, kidneys and heart were all eaten. Oil from the blubber was burned for light and heat. Bones were used for building materials and carved into tools and ornaments, while baleen was made into fishing nets and the ribs of skin boats. The Inuit even found a use for the thin outer layer of the whale's liver - it became the skin of a drum

Commercial whaling

The Inuit were not commercial whalers, for they hunted whales solely for their own use. The first people to hunt whales for money were the Basques, the people who live on the Bay of Biscay, at the border of Spain and France.

In the 1100s, the Basques were hunting a smaller relative of the bowhead, the right whale, so called because it was the 'right whale to hunt'. Like the bowhead, it is slow swimming and so rich in blubber that it floats when it is killed.

Each October, right whales arrived from the north to spend the winter in the Bay of Biscay.

Everyone in the Inuit village helps to cut the whale up. The meat will last for months.

Right Working to the music of a bagpiper, Basque whalers cut up a right whale. The artist who drew this scene, in the early 1500s, had obviously never seen a whale!

Along the coast, there were stone watchtowers, where look-outs scanned the sea. As soon as a whale was seen, the look-out set fire to a pile of wet straw at the top of the tower. This smoke signal brought the fishermen running from all parts of the town. To the sound of a drum, they set off in tiny wooden boats to attack the whales.

The boats worked together, herding the whales and cutting off their retreat into the open sea. The men killed the whales with harpoons, and then dragged them ashore. Here the blubber was boiled in great pots, to extract the oil. This was sold, to be burned in oil lamps - mainly in churches and public buildings. The whale's tongue - considered a great delicacy - was given to the local lords.

The Basques were so efficient that they wiped out their own supply of whales. In order to carry on hunting, they had to build large sea-going ships and set off across the North Atlantic. In the 1500s, they found a new source of whales off the coast of Canada. But the right whales never came back to the Bay of Biscay.

Above Dutch whalers, in the 1700s, boiling blubber in an enormous cauldron.

Below In the 1600s, the Dutch began catching bowhead whales around the island of Spitsbergen, north of Norway. They built a town there, called Smeerenburg (Blubbertown). Deserted each winter, it came to life again in the summer when thousands of whalers, shop-keepers and craftspeople arrived. Then, one day, there were no more whales left to hunt.

HUNTING THE SPERM WHALE

OFF the coast of New England in North America, there is a small island called Nantucket. It was settled by Europeans in 1659, who soon found that fishing was the only way of making a living there. Nothing would grow in its sandy soil. On the mainland, people told jokes about this sea-soaked island. They said that the Nantucketers had to pull shellfish off their chairs and tables before they could sit down to dinner.

To begin with, the islanders hunted right whales, which they found close to the coast. But then, in 1712, something happened which completely changed the Nantucketers' way of life. Captain Christopher Hussey was hunting right whales when his ship was blown out to sea by a sudden gale. As the weather cleared, he saw whales spouting in the distance. Hussey could see that they were not right whales, for they have a high double spout. These whales had a single low spout, but he decided to go after them anyway.

Right whale

Sperm whale

Minke whale

Different types of whale can be recognized by the shape of their spouts. From the left, you can see a right, a sperm, a minke, a sei and a humpback whale.

10

Hussey harpooned a whale, which put up a much harder fight than he was used to. Even so, he was able to kill it and tow it to the shore. It was a peculiar looking creature, with a huge square head and teeth, rather than baleen plates. It was a sperm whale.

A sperm whale, its huge head rising from the water, is an awesome sight.

Blubber

Oil

Spermaceti

Blowhole

Whales into candles

Imagine the astonishment of those whalers, when they cut open the sperm whale's head and found it full of oil and a type of wax called spermaceti. There was so much of it that they had to bale it out with buckets. This was the whale to hunt!

By the 1750s, the Nantucket islanders were making candles from spermaceti. Unlike tallow (animal fat) candles, these burned with a brilliant smokeless flame. They were immediately popular. Soon the Nantucket workshops were turning out vast numbers of them, to be sold on the mainland and shipped to Europe.

To meet the demand for oil and spermaceti, the whalers sailed further into the Atlantic and used bigger ships that could carry more blubber back to the Nantucket furnaces.

The head of a sperm whale. These whales have less blubber than right whales, but their oil is of a very high quality. It burns brightly, without the nasty smell given off by right whale oil. The huge head is full of a mixture of this oil and spermaceti.

Sei whale

Humpback whale

A box of spermaceti candles made in New Bedford

Then, some time in the 1750s, the Nantucketers made a big step forward: they began to build brick furnaces on the decks of their ships. Once they could boil the blubber at sea, they had no need to return home until their holds were full. They were able to sail all around the world after sperm whales, on voyages lasting up to four years.

The docks of New Bedford, crammed with barrels of sperm whale oil. By the 1850s, New Bedford was the whaling capital of the world.

Around the world after sperm whales

The whalers found that they were most likely to come across sperm whales in certain areas of the ocean, which they called the 'sperm whaling grounds'.

The map shows a typical whaling voyage of the nineteenth century. The ship sailed from New England, heading first east to the Azores and then south to Cape Horn, at the tip of South America. After rounding this stormy cape, it would sail into the Pacific, up the coast of Chile.

There were many different routes in the Pacific. Some ships headed south, to New Zealand and Australia. Others sailed north, to the Bering Sea, to hunt the slow-moving bowheads. The choice depended on the weather or on news of whales from other ships. One year's good hunting ground might have no whales the following year. Whichever route was taken, between two and four years after setting off, the ship would be back home, packed with barrels of oil.

Below When they saw the profits that Nantucket was making, the other ports of New England turned to whaling. The most important was New Bedford, which had a bigger, deeper harbour than Nantucket and could take larger ships. By the 1850s, half of all American whaling ships were based in New Bedford.

Below Hunting sperm whales in the South Pacific

New England Whaling Ports

Boston
Provincetown
New Bedford
Fairhaven
New London
Mystic
Newport
Stonington
Nantucket
Sag Harbour

Sperm whaling grounds
Typical whaling voyage

ASIA
NORTH AMERICA
Azores
EUROPE
AFRICA
SOUTH AMERICA
Australia
Pacific Ocean
Atlantic Ocean
Indian Ocean

A Whaling Voyage

LIFE ON A WHALING SHIP

Valued for his skills, a harpooner was often paid twice as much as the ordinary sailors.

WHALING was tough, dangerous and badly paid. Apart from the ship's officers and the harpooners, most of the crew were not professional sailors. They were often men who were desperate for work, such as escaped black slaves from the South or bankrupt shop-keepers. There were also young farm boys, looking for adventure. Recruiting agents in the towns of the east coast gave them a glowing picture of life on a whaler.

In his 1846 book, *Etchings of a Whaling Cruise*, John Ross Browne describes how he was recruited. The agent described the joys of a whaling voyage: 'Whaling, gentlemen, is tolerably hard at first, but it's the finest business in the world for enterprising young men … Vigilance and activity will insure you rapid promotion … A whaler, gentlemen, is a place of refuge for the distressed … There's nothing like it. You can see the world; you can see something of life!'

More sailors were hired on the voyage, in the Azores and the Cape Verde Islands. The black Cape Verdean Islanders were particularly famous for their skill as harpooners.

As the ship sailed on, some sailors deserted or died. They were replaced by Chileans, South Sea Islanders, Australians, and Maoris from New Zealand. A whaling crew was truly international.

Payment

The men were not paid fixed wages. Instead, they got a 'lay', or share, of the value of the whale oil at the end of the voyage. This was supposed to make them work harder and take more risks in catching whales. The system also benefited the ship's owners. If oil prices dropped, or if few whales had been caught, the ordinary sailors lost their money.

The dangers of whaling are clear in this 1852 print. Two ships, crushed in the ice, have had to be burned to avoid danger to the third ship. It will be a cramped voyage home!

An American whaler

This is a cross-section of a typical nineteenth-century American whaling ship - the sturdiest type of sailing ship ever built. It had a broad hull, built of heavy timbers. A whaler had to be strong and stable, for it took enormous strain when the blubber from a dead whale was winched aboard. It also spent much longer at sea than other ships, standing up to all kinds of bad weather.

Spending so long at sea, the ship needed to carry carpenter's and blacksmith's tools, to make repairs, as well as spares for everything - spare boats, spare harpoons, spare ropes, 'spare everythings almost,' wrote the ex-whaler Herman Melville, 'but a spare Captain and a duplicate ship'. The deck was cluttered with equipment.

Near the front of the deck, you can see a strange-looking brick structure. This is the try-works, where the whale blubber was boiled to extract the oil. Another odd feature is the cutting stage. This was a wooden platform that was lowered for the men to stand on while they butchered the whale.

Sailors on the slim, fast merchant ships made fun of the 'blubber hunters', as they called the whalers. They said that they were 'built by the mile', with each ship chopped off, like a sausage. As well as looking clumsy, whaling ships were slow. But, unlike merchant ships, they had no need to reach any particular port in a hurry. In fact, whaling captains preferred to avoid ports, because large numbers of the crew would desert.

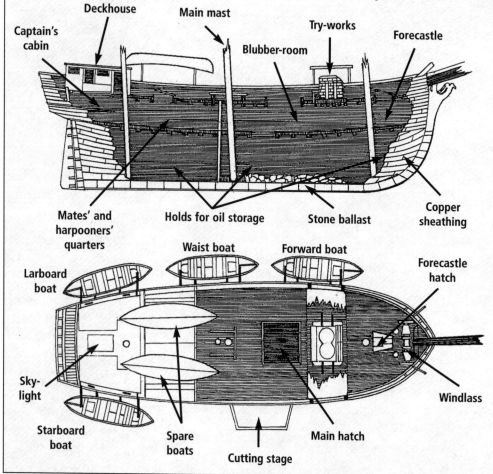

Deckhouse · Main mast · Try-works · Forecastle · Captain's cabin · Blubber-room · Mates' and harpooners' quarters · Holds for oil storage · Stone ballast · Copper sheathing · Larboard boat · Waist boat · Forward boat · Forecastle hatch · Sky-light · Starboard boat · Spare boats · Cutting stage · Main hatch · Windlass

Below The *Charles W. Morgan*, was one of the last American whaling ships. It is now open as a museum in Mystic, Connecticut, USA.

Tied to the rigging and flogged with a length of tarred rope - a common punishment on board a whaling ship.

First days at sea

New sailors usually spent their first days at sea being sick over the side, until they got used to the rocking of the ship. This was called 'getting their sea legs'. Meanwhile, they were forced to hoist sails and scrub the decks. Discipline was harsh, for the ship's officers were determined to turn the men into sailors. Men who disobeyed orders were flogged. Frank Bullen remembers this time on his own ship: 'The black portion of the crew - Portuguese natives [Cape Verdean Islanders] - were doing their work all right … but the farmers, and bakers, and draymen were being driven about mercilessly … As night fell, the condition of the 'greenies', or non-sailor portion of the crew, was pitiable. Helpless from sea-sickness, not knowing where to go or what to do, bullied relentlessly by the ruthless petty officers …'

Many sailors became skilled at carving whalebone and sperm whale teeth. This decorative work was called 'scrimshaw'. On the teeth, they cut whaling scenes and pictures of loved ones back home.

Yarns and songs

The sailors relaxed by 'spinning yarns', or telling stories. These were often tales about whaling adventures, but ghost and murder

yarns were especially popular. There was also music, played on whistles, fiddles, guitars and squeeze boxes. The men sang songs, many of them made up by whalers and passed from ship to ship.

The cramped forecastle of an American whaler, home to the men for up to four years.

Below Some whaling captains took their wives to sea with them. It must have been a strange life for these women. This is Carrie Nye Sherman with her baby, Helen, who was born on her husband's whaling ship in 1894.

In the forecastle

While the captain, the mates and harpooners lived at the rear, or stern, of the ship, the ordinary sailors lived in the forecastle, a small dark room beneath the deck at the bow. John Ross Browne described the forecastle on his whaling ship: 'The forecastle was black and slimy with filth, very small and hot as an oven. It was filled with … foul air, smoke, sea-chests, soap-kegs, greasy pans, tainted meat, Portuguese ruffians and sea-sick Americans.'

The food they ate was disgusting. The usual meal, eaten day after day, was salted meat and hard dried bread, which might be crawling with maggots. The men drank tea or, as Browne remembered, 'boiled weeds and molasses as a substitute for tea and sugar'.

The crews of two whalers gather around the windlass for a 'gam'. Can you see the man on the left reading a letter? Whaling ships often carried mail from home for other ships they expected to meet.

Gamming

The biggest social event on a whaling ship was a 'gam'. This was when two ships met in mid-ocean, and the crew of one paid a visit to the other. While the captains discussed whaling, the men danced, sang and spun yarns.

One of the most popular songs, first sung around 1800, was 'The Greenland Whale Fishery'. It tells the story of a voyage to Greenland, 'where there's ice and snow and the whale fishes blow.' Here are two verses, about a disastrous meeting with a whale:

The harpoon struck and the line paid out,
With a single flourish of his tail,
He capsized the boat and we lost five men,
And we did not catch the whale, brave boys,
And we did not catch the whale.

Now the losing of the five jolly men,
It grieved our captain sore.
But the losing of that fine whale fish,
It grieved him ten times more, brave boys,
It grieved him ten times more.

Two American whalers meet in mid-ocean for a 'gam'. Everybody looked forward to such meetings. A 'gam' meant news from the outside world and a break in the usual boring routine of life on board.

HOW DID THEY KILL A WHALE?

About 30 m above the deck, with the mast at an alarming angle, the look-out sings out. He has seen a sperm whale in the distance.

AS the ship slowly sailed across the sea, a look-out was sent up the main mast. The man stood high up on a tiny platform, inside a padded metal hoop just above his waist. Leaning on this hoop, with the ship rolling beneath him, he watched the wide blue sea for sperm whales.

There she blows!

For days, there might be no sign of a whale, or the men might see blue or fin whales - identified by a high straight spout. These whales were too fast to be caught, and the look-outs learned to ignore them. Eventually, however, a look-out would see in the distance a whale with a low bushy spout - the spout of a sperm whale. John Ross Browne described what happened next:

'There she blows!' was sung out from the mast-head.

'Where away?' demanded the captain.

'Three points off the lee bow, sir …

'Mast-head ahoy! Do you see that whale now?'

'Ay, ay, sir! A school of sperm whales! There she blows! There she breaches!'

'Sing out! Sing out every time!'

'Ay, ay, sir! There she blows! There - there - thar' she blows - bowes - bo-o-o-s!'

20

At the first shout from the mast-head, the men raced to the whaleboats, where they waited for the captain's order to 'lower away!' Then the boats were dropped over the side, the men leaping in after.

These whale-boats are pausing in the chase. The whales have 'sounded', or dived below the surface. The men wait for them to reappear.

The chase

Each whaleboat had a small mast and a sail, so that the men could sail most of the way to the whale. When they got close, the mast was taken down and the men took up their oars. Each boat carried five oarsmen, including the harpooner. The sixth man was the 'boat-header' - the captain or one of the mates - who stood at the rear of the boat, steering with a long oar. When the whales disappeared below the surface, he had to guess where they were likely to come up again, and steer the boat there. The oarsmen rowed facing the boat-header, who bellowed at them to row harder.

Approaching the whale, the oarsmen pull even harder. The harpooner prepares to strike.

Hunting right whales in the South Pacific. These gentle animals were much easier to kill than sperm whales.

Simply rowing the boat was exhausting, but the harpooner had to do much more. Once they were close enough to the whale, the boat-header would shout, 'Stand up and give it to him!' At this, the harpooner dropped his oar and jumped to his feet. Standing in the swaying boat, he hurled his harpoon at the whale with all his strength.

Hit by the harpoon, the terrified whale dived or raced away. The harpoon rope whistled through the air, unwinding from its tub in the rear of the boat. This was a dangerous moment for the men. If they got in the way of the rope, they could lose an arm, or be dragged overboard.

The Nantucket sleigh-ride

The wounded whale raced along, dragging the boat behind it at 25 km an hour, while the men gripped the sides and kept their heads down. This headlong dash, nicknamed the 'Nantucket sleigh-ride', was described by Frank Bullen: 'The whale started off to windward with us at a tremendous rate … The speed at which he went made it seem as if a gale of wind was blowing, and we flew along the sea surface, leaping from crest to crest of the waves … The flying spray drenched us and prevented us from seeing him …'

Eventually, the whale became tired and slowed down. Now the men pulled on the rope, hauling themselves closer and closer.

A sperm whale races off, dragging the whale-boat behind it. One man pours water over the rope to stop it bursting into flames. But the sea is becoming too rough, and so the man with the axe is getting ready to cut the whale free.

Right Whaling harpoons had barbed iron points and heavy wooden handles.

Above Here is some of the equipment that each whaleboat carried. It included oars, harpoons, a big tub for the whale-line, buckets for baling out water, and a keg of drinking water.

Right A lance, the weapon used by the boat-header to finish off the whale.

At this point, the boat-header and the harpooner had to swap places. It was the boat-header's job to kill the whale. This was a difficult task, and he was the most experienced man.

The kill

The killing of the whale was another dangerous time for the men. The boat had to get in close, where it could easily be smashed by the whale's thrashing tail. The boat-header used a long lance which he plunged into the whale's side, aiming to hit the lungs or heart. Unlike the barbed harpoon, the lance point had a rounded edge, like a spoon. This was so it could be pulled out and thrust in, again and again, until the whale was killed.

Now the whale would thrash wildly as it went into a 'flurry', or death agony. At last, it rolled on to its side, dead. For the first time, the men could relax. While the dead whale bobbed alongside, they sat back, got out their clay pipes, and had a smoke.

The huge sperm whale rolls over, dead. Thrashing in its final agony, it has smashed one of the whaleboats.

WHAT DID THEY DO WITH THE DEAD WHALE?

THE killing of the whale was just the beginning of the hard work. First, the huge animal was slowly towed back to the ship, where it was fastened by a chain around its tail. Now the blubber had to be cut from the whale and lifted on board. This job was called 'cutting in'.

Whalers off the coast of Greenland, in around 1800. The whale's body is pulled alongside the ship and the 'cutting in' has started.

On the right, the men turn the windlass which pulls the blubber into the air. Meanwhile, the mates and harpooners cut with their long-handled spades. Accidents were common during cutting in, for the men were working with razor-sharp tools on the slippery deck of a rolling ship.

Cutting in

Like all skilled whaling work, the cutting in was done by the most experienced men - the mates and harpooners. They worked on the cutting stage, the wooden platform over the whale, sometimes jumping down to balance on its back. The ordinary crewmen raised the blubber on board. They did this by turning the windlass, the big winch at the bow (front) of the ship.

First, the mates cut a hole in the side of the whale, just above the fin. Then one of the harpooners jumped on to the animal, and stuck a big metal hook into this hole. Ropes from the hook passed through a pulley on the mast to the windlass. Here six to eight men worked together, pushing to the rhythm of a song called a 'sea shanty'.

As the men sang and pushed at the windlass, the mates cut at the side of the whale with their long-handled spades. For a while, the ship would tilt over at an alarming angle. Then, with a loud snap, the blubber began to come free and the ship rolled upright. The blubber was ripped off in a continuous strip, while the body of the whale turned round and round. The whale was peeled rather like an orange.

Down to the blubber-room

Once the strip of blubber had been lifted as high as it could go, the harpooners had to slice off the bottom end of it using a long knife. They lowered the sliced-off strip through a big hatch on the deck, down to the blubber-room. Here, crewmen cut it into small blocks called 'horse pieces'. This was a filthy job, and the blubber-room men were soaked from head to foot in oil.

A sperm whale was always cut up in the same way, as shown in this diagram.

By now, the whole deck was swimming in blood and oil, which gushed like water from the blubber. None of this oil was allowed to escape. The 'scupper holes' that drained the deck were blocked up and men crawled about, sponging up the oil with rags and scoops.

From time to time, the men found lumps of a grey waxy substance in a sperm whale's guts. This was called ambergris and it was extremely valuable. When it dried out, it gave off a sweet scent and it was used in the making of perfume.

Trying-out

From the blubber room, the horse pieces were sent back up on deck. Here they were deeply scored with a knife. The thin slices were nicknamed 'Bible leaves', for they looked like the pages of a book. They were ready for boiling, or 'trying-out'.

The harpooners tossed the blubber into round iron pots in the try-works, the brick furnace on the deck of the ship.

This man is lifting pieces of blubber out of the pots in the try-works after the oil has been extracted from them. For days and nights, the fire was kept burning and the air was filled with stinking smoke. Everything became coated with soot. On a dark night, the smoke and the red glow of the fire made a striking scene. John Ross Browne compared it to 'hell on a small scale'.

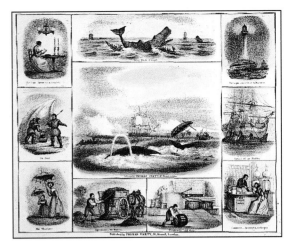

Right This engraving shows just some of the nineteenth century uses of whale products - spermaceti candles, lighting oil, oil used in industry, perfume, manure, baleen for umbrella ribs and food for the Inuit.

To begin with, they fed its fire with wood. But then the first crisped scraps of blubber were fished out of the bubbling oil and thrown into the flames. Once these started burning, no more wood was needed. 'The whale supplies his own fuel,' wrote Herman Melville, 'and burns by his own body.' The oil was ladled into a cooling tank. Finally, it was piped through a canvas hose into barrels in the hold. When all the oil had been extracted from the blubber, the men scrubbed the ship clean and got ready to start all over again with the next whale.

Baling the case

There was one other big job - getting the oil and spermaceti wax out of the whale's head. This had been chopped off at the start of cutting in and tied from the stern (back) of the ship until it could be dealt with. With a small whale, the head was heaved on to the deck and cut open.

With a big whale, the head was lifted partly out of the sea. A harpooner had to go over the side and stand on the head, baling the stuff out with a bucket on a long pole. This was called 'baling the case'. A single whale's head could fill fifteen oil barrels.

The men wade up to their knees in the whale's head, scooping up the spermaceti.

DID WHALES EVER FIGHT BACK?

THE most famous whale of all appears in Herman Melville's 1851 novel, *Moby-Dick*. This tells the story of the crazed Captain Ahab and his hunt for a great white sperm whale called Moby-Dick. Moby-Dick is a terrifying monster, with a row of twisted harpoons stuck in his side, signs of his many battles with whalers. During one such battle, he has ripped off Captain Ahab's leg. Now Ahab has only one aim in life - revenge. Ahab's ship, the *Pequod*, sails the world's oceans, from one fishing ground to another, searching for the white whale. But it is not until Chapter 133 that the long-awaited shout is heard from the look-out: 'There she blows! A hump like a snow-hill! It is Moby-Dick!'

Many whalers lost their lives in scenes like this, far from home.

Gregory Peck as Captain Ahab, in the film of *Moby-Dick*. Ahab is making a last, desperate effort to kill Moby-Dick. The whale's side is riddled with harpoons - evidence of many other attacks that have failed. Ahab's missing left leg has been replaced with an artificial one made from the jaw of a sperm whale.

A three-day chase follows, which ends when Moby-Dick rams and sinks the *Pequod*. Ahab harpoons the whale, but he becomes tangled in the rope and is dragged to his death. The white whale lives to fight again.

The idea of a whale attacking a ship seems hard to believe. But Melville knew what he was writing about. As a young man, he had served on a whaler and he had heard many stories of fighting whales. The sailors often gave these whales nicknames, like 'Timor Jack', 'Mocha Dick' and 'New Zealand Tom'. Melville's novel is based on these stories.

Above One of the *Pequod*'s boats gives chase, in an illustration from *Moby-Dick*. 'Pull, pull!', cries Starbuck, the first mate.

The wreck of the *Essex*

Melville based the sinking of the *Pequod* on a real event. On 20 November 1820, the whaling ship *Essex* came upon a group of sperm whales in the South Pacific. The ship's boats were launched and the hunt began. The first mate, Owen Chase, harpooned a whale which thrashed with its tail, smashing a hole in his boat. Chase managed to stuff some jackets into the hole, and got back to the ship.

A smashed whaleboat was nothing unusual to Owen Chase. But what he saw next astonished him. An enormous bull whale had appeared close by and was making straight for the *Essex*. Chase later recalled: 'He came down upon us with full speed, and struck the ship with his head … he gave us such an appalling and tremendous jar, as nearly threw us all on our faces.'

A whale's powerful tail could be a dangerous weapon, flicking a boat right out of the water.

The loss of the whaling ship *Essex*. This picture is a scene from a panorama called *A Whaling Voyage Around the World*. The panorama, which is over 380 m long, was painted in 1847-48 by two men from the American whaling port of New Bedford.

The ship had been holed, and Chase gave orders to start pumping out the water. But, minutes later, one of the crew shouted, 'Here he is - he is making for us again!'.

'I turned around, and saw him … coming down apparently with twice his ordinary speed, and to me at that moment, it appeared with ten-fold fury and vengeance … The surf flew in all directions about him, and his course towards us was marked by a white foam … which he made with the continual violent thrashing of his tail; his head was about half out of the water, and in that way … he came upon, and again struck the ship.'

Below In *Moby-Dick*, Herman Melville praises this painting of a whaling disaster by the French artist, Louis Garneray. He describes it as 'wonderfully good and true', adding that 'the French are the lads for the painting action'.

Sperm whales were sometimes known to crush the fragile whaleboats between their jaws. This picture comes from Frank Bullen's book, *The Cruise of the Cachalot*, in which he describes such an attack.

The ship was now so badly damaged that the men had to abandon her. By the time the two other whaling boats returned from the hunt, most of the *Essex* was below the water. Imagine how the men felt when they saw what had happened! They were almost 2,000 km from land, with just three small boats and few supplies.

A terrible voyage lay ahead of them. One by one, they died of thirst and hunger. Of twenty crewmen, only eight survived - by eating their dead shipmates.

Mocha Dick, terror whale of the Pacific

While Melville was writing his novel, there was a real white sperm whale living in the Pacific Ocean. He was first seen around 1810, near the island of Mocha, off the coast of Chile. From this came his nickname, 'Mocha Dick'.

Between 1810 and 1859, Mocha Dick was said to have smashed fourteen whaleboats, killing thirty men. He was also blamed for sinking three ships, and badly damaging three others. Among the whalers, he became so famous that they would greet each other with

cries of 'Any news from Mocha Dick?'

Mocha Dick was finally killed in August 1859, off the coast of Brazil. The Swedish whalers who caught him said that he put up very little of a fight, but by now he was a very old whale. They measured him and found that he was 30 m long (sperm whales are rarely bigger than 18 m). His huge head was covered with scars and he was blind in one eye. When they cut him open, they found the iron points from nineteen harpoons buried in his body.

WHAT IS MODERN WHALING?

B Y the 1860s, the whaling business was in trouble. Whales no longer provided the main oil used in lighting and industry. Now there were also fossil fuels, such as petroleum and coal gas; and vegetable oils made from linseed and cotton-seed. These were all cheaper to produce than whale oil.

There was still a big demand for baleen, from bowheads and right whales, for corsets, brushes and umbrellas. The problem was that the bow-heads and the right whales had been almost wiped out by hunting.

How do you catch a rorqual?

One group of whales had never been hunted. These were the rorquals, the family including the blue, fin, minke, sei, Bryde's and humpback whales. Rorquals are the fastest whales. The fin whale, for example, races along at over 40 km/h. It is nicknamed, 'the greyhound of the sea'. A rowing boat had no chance of chasing a rorqual down.

Rorqual whales all share the same long, slim shape. This makes them much faster than other whales. The biggest rorqual is the blue whale, the largest animal that has ever lived on our planet. At birth, it is already seven metres long and weighs eight tonnes. It can grow to 33 metres and weigh 190 tonnes - the same as twenty-five elephants.

Humpback whale

Sei whale

Bryde's whale

Fin whale

Blue whale

Minke whale

Rorquals are also extremely strong. If a whaler got close enough to harpoon one, it would quickly take all his line and break it. Yet another problem is that, unlike sperm and right whales, rorquals sink when they die.

It is not surprising that the hunters had left them alone. Yet, if whaling was to have any future, a way had to be found to catch rorquals. For they were the only whales left in large numbers.

The harpoon cannon

The problem of hunting rorquals was solved by a Norwegian seal hunter, called Svend Foyn. Sailing along the coast of Norway, he often watched these fast whales swimming beside his boat. Foyn, who was very religious, said that God had put the whales there 'for the benefit and blessing of mankind.' He decided that it was his mission to find a way to catch them.

In the 1860s, Foyn invented a completely new way of catching whales. Instead of chasing whales in a small rowing boat, he built a steam-powered 'catcher boat'. On its deck, he set up a cannon, which fired a harpoon with an exploding shell. The harpoon had steel barbs, which swung open when

The harpoon cannon invented by the Norwegian Svend Foyn. It enabled whalers to hunt and kill all types of whales, even the fastest and strongest of the rorquals.

Pumped full of air, a rorqual is towed to a processing station on the coast of Norway. You can see the folds of skin on the whale's belly which give it its name. Rorqual means 'whale with pleats'.

the whale tugged on the line, fastening it in its side. The barbs also acted as a trigger, setting off an explosion inside the whale's body.

When the dead whale sank, Foyn used a steam-powered winch to haul it to the surface. It was then towed to the shore to be processed. Later, in the 1880s, he began to pump air into the dead whales to keep them afloat.

Struggle to the death

A scientist called Herman Sandburg watched the hunt for a blue whale on Foyn's boat: 'We came close to the whale, which was clearly not the least bit afraid of us. It was almost as long as the boat, and much wide ... The shot was fired. The harpoon immediately disappeared inside the body of the whale ... We all thought that the animal had been instantly killed, but immediately afterwards it dived, the line ran taut, and a muffled report told us that the shell had exploded inside the whale. Once again it stopped, as though struck by lightning. But now the wild chase began. Maddened with pain, the whale darted hither and thither, now diving into the sea, now surfacing ... The whale stained the sea red in a wide circle around it, and spouted great columns of blood every time it surfaced. The struggle lasted nearly an hour, until the whale was finally exhausted.'

Whales had no chance of escape from a steam-powered catcher boat armed with a harpoon cannon.

For the hunters, Svend Foyn had ended the dangers of whaling. There would no longer be smashed boats, or men dragged overboard by harpoon lines. The age of modern whaling had begun.

The Antarctic

The best place to hunt rorquals was in the icy seas around Antarctica. In summer, the waters here swarm with a pink shrimp called krill. Hundreds of thousands of rorquals went there each summer to feed on the krill. Far from land, or sailing routes, this was the one place where whales had always been safe from hunting.

These krill are found in such huge numbers in the Antarctic that they can make the water appear pink.

Left High above the whale, the gunner has plenty of time to take aim and fire. One harpoon has already hit the whale; another is in flight.

Top A harpooned fin whale makes a desperate attempt to escape.

38

Factory ships

Apart from the lonely island of South Georgia, there were few places in the Antarctic to build whaling stations. The whalers' answer was the 'floating factory'. This was a big ship, able to process whales caught by small chaser boats.

The first floating factories, in the early 1900s, were converted cargo ships. Then, in 1925, the whalers began to use specially designed ships with a huge ramp at the stern. The whale was dragged up the ramp on to the deck by motorized winches. It was cut up and the blubber and bones were boiled together to extract the oil. Leftover bones were ground up for animal food and fertiliser. It took less than an hour to process a full-sized blue whale. Nothing was wasted.

The lonely whaling station at Gritviken, South Georgia. Now abandoned, the old catcher boats rot in the harbour. In 1930-31, when there were 41 factory ships in the Antarctic, 29,410 blue whales were killed. The blue whales began to disappear from the oceans, just like the bowheads and the right whales before them.

Medicine, margarine and meat

By the 1920s, there was no longer a demand for baleen corsets or for whale oil as a lighting fuel. However, scientists found many new uses for dead whales. They used extracts from the glands for medicines - for arthritis, rheumatism and diabetes. With a new chemical process called hydrogenation, they were able to change whale oil into margarine and high-quality soap. In the 1930s, more than 80 per cent of whale oil was turned into margarine. A by-product of making the soap was a liquid called glycerine, used to make explosives.

The whalers also tried to sell the meat for food, marketing it as 'sea beef'. When the usual meat products were scarce, following the Second World War of 1939-45, whalemeat did sell. Mrs Vera Mather, an English housewife, tried it once: 'It was … terribly smelly, and it didn't taste like anything, it was neither fish nor meat … We had it once but you could smell it right through the house for a whole week afterwards.'

Although whalemeat was unpopular in most countries, the Japanese loved it. They ate almost every part of a rorqual, including its skin, gums and lungs. However, they would only eat the tail of a sperm whale. Sperm whales are said to taste horrible.

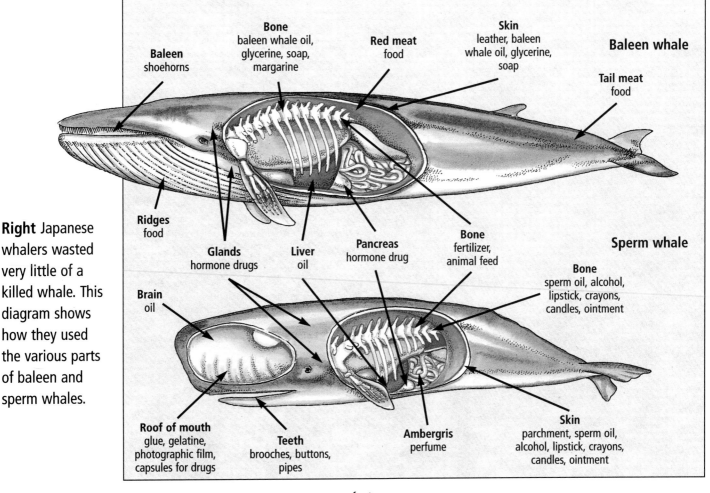

Baleen whale

Baleen shoehorns

Bone baleen whale oil, glycerine, soap, margarine

Red meat food

Skin leather, baleen whale oil, glycerine, soap

Tail meat food

Ridges food

Glands hormone drugs

Liver oil

Pancreas hormone drug

Bone fertilizer, animal feed

Sperm whale

Bone sperm oil, alcohol, lipstick, crayons, candles, ointment

Brain oil

Roof of mouth glue, gelatine, photographic film, capsules for drugs

Teeth brooches, buttons, pipes

Ambergris perfume

Skin parchment, sperm oil, alcohol, lipstick, crayons, candles, ointment

WILL WHALES SURVIVE?

O N 27 June 1975, a Soviet factory ship was hunting sperm whales in the Pacific Ocean. One of its catcher boats, chasing a group of whales, was just about to fire its harpoon cannon, when three small rubber speed-boats appeared, coming between the gunner and the fleeing whales.

In the speed-boats were members of Greenpeace, an organization formed in 1970 to draw attention to the different ways in which we are damaging our world. One of their campaigns was against the hunting of whales. The protesters in the rubber boats hoped that the Soviet gunner would not fire if he risked hitting people. However, he simply fired over their heads and killed two whales.

In their tiny inflatable speed-boat, Greenpeace protesters race towards a Soviet factory ship.

The power of television

Although the protesters had not saved the whales, they filmed the whole event. Their film was shown on news programmes around the world.

A small pilot whale swims gracefully through the water. Underwater photography led to a new understanding of whales.

Robert Hunter, the leader of the expedition, later wrote that this film changed people's idea of what whaling meant: 'Instead of small boats and giant whales, giant boats and small whales; instead of courage killing whales, courage saving whales.'

At the same time people's attitude to the whales themselves was changing, thanks to television documentaries. On television, they could see the grace of whales swimming in their underwater world. A top-selling record of 1970 played a similar role. It was a recording of the songs of male humpback whales. People were astonished when they heard the whales' beautiful, eerie moans, clicks, whistles and roars. It seemed that whales lived much more complex and strange lives than anyone had ever realized.

More and more, whales came to be seen as special animals that deserved protection. Gregory Peck, the actor who had played Captain Ahab in the film of *Moby-Dick*, summed up this new attitude to whaling: 'There are cheap, plentiful substitutes for all whale products. Unfortunately, there are no substitutes for whales.'

A Japanese factory ship hauls a dead minke whale on board.

The International Whaling Commission

By the 1930s, the leading whaling nations saw that hunting had to be controlled. If the whaling industry itself did not limit the killing, there would soon be no whales left to kill. In 1946, the whaling nations joined together to form the International Whaling Commission (IWC). They agreed to set quotas - numbers of each sort of whale that could be killed. They also banned the killing of baby whales and nursing mothers, and limited hunting to certain seasons of the year.

The biggest problem was getting the members to agree on low enough quotas. Despite the IWC, between 1950 and 1985, more whales were killed than ever before.

The end of commercial whaling?

This Inuit in a kayak is hunting a narwhal. The Inuit kill around 1,000 of these small whales each year.

After years arguing over quotas, in 1982, the IWC voted to have a moratorium, or temporary ban, on all commercial whaling until stocks of whales recovered. This did not mean that all whale hunting ended. Because of a loop-hole, Japan, Norway and Iceland each continued to kill a few hundred minke and sei whales a year for what were called 'research purposes'. The Inuit of Alaska were also allowed to carry on their traditional hunting of small numbers of bowheads.

In the 1950s, a new type of whaling ship appeared on the seas, the pirate whaler. This was a ship that killed every sort of whale, in and out of season. The *Sierra* (above) was a pirate that began to hunt whales in 1968. It was both a catcher boat and a small factory ship. It killed whales solely for the tail meat, which was sold to Japan; the rest of the whale's body was dumped. The *Sierra*, was blown up and sunk by anti-whaling protesters in 1980.

There has been no large-scale whaling since 1986, when the moratorium began. However, for some types of whales, the ban may have come too late. Before the whalers arrived in the Antarctic, at the start of the twentieth century, it was home to 250,000 blue whales. In July 1994, the IWC estimated that there were only 460 of them left.

Whale-watching

In California, whale-watchers are able to lean out of their boats and touch the grey whales.

Human greed was always the whales' worst enemy. But nowadays, it is possible to make money from whales without killing them. Many of the places that used to kill whales now earn large sums by showing them to tourists on whale-watching trips. In South Australia, for example, you can see right whales in their winter breeding grounds. Off the coasts of California and eastern Canada, you can watch the liveliest whale of all, the humpback, which is famous for its huge leaps out of the water. All over the world, whales are now astonishing people on whale-watching trips. Perhaps, for the first time ever, living whales are worth more than dead ones.

Humpback whales can leap right out of the water. Imagine seeing this from a small boat!

TIMELINE

AD 1850   **1900**   **1950**

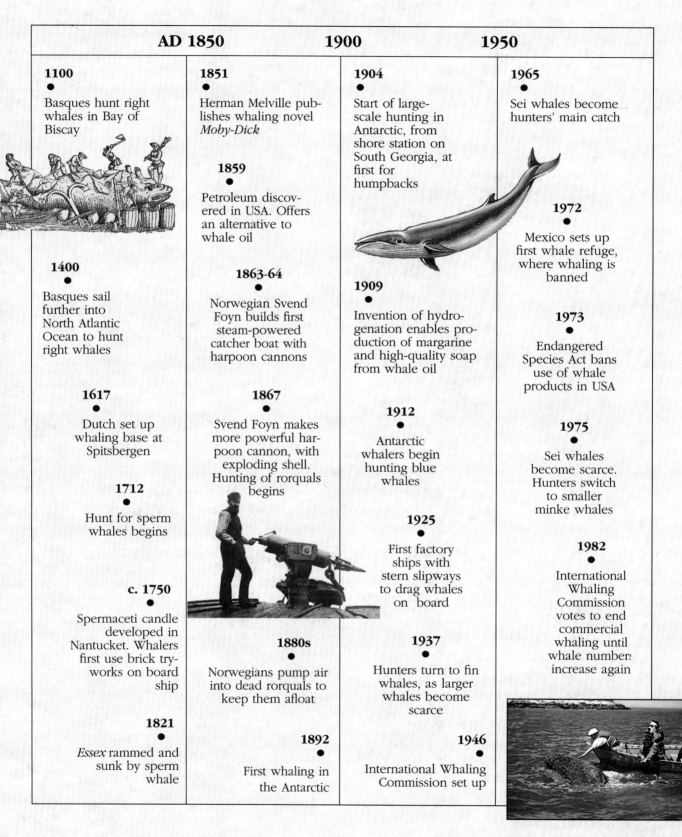

1100
●
Basques hunt right whales in Bay of Biscay

1400
●
Basques sail further into North Atlantic Ocean to hunt right whales

1617
●
Dutch set up whaling base at Spitsbergen

1712
●
Hunt for sperm whales begins

c. 1750
●
Spermaceti candle developed in Nantucket. Whalers first use brick try-works on board ship

1821
●
Essex rammed and sunk by sperm whale

1851
●
Herman Melville publishes whaling novel *Moby-Dick*

1859
●
Petroleum discovered in USA. Offers an alternative to whale oil

1863-64
●
Norwegian Svend Foyn builds first steam-powered catcher boat with harpoon cannons

1867
●
Svend Foyn makes more powerful harpoon cannon, with exploding shell. Hunting of rorquals begins

1880s
●
Norwegians pump air into dead rorquals to keep them afloat

1892
●
First whaling in the Antarctic

1904
●
Start of large-scale hunting in Antarctic, from shore station on South Georgia, at first for humpbacks

1909
●
Invention of hydrogenation enables production of margarine and high-quality soap from whale oil

1912
●
Antarctic whalers begin hunting blue whales

1925
●
First factory ships with stern slipways to drag whales on board

1937
●
Hunters turn to fin whales, as larger whales become scarce

1946
●
International Whaling Commission set up

1965
●
Sei whales become hunters' main catch

1972
●
Mexico sets up first whale refuge, where whaling is banned

1973
●
Endangered Species Act bans use of whale products in USA

1975
●
Sei whales become scarce. Hunters switch to smaller minke whales

1982
●
International Whaling Commission votes to end commercial whaling until whale numbers increase again

GLOSSARY

Ambergris A waxy substance, occasionally found in the intestines of a sperm whale. Used in the making of perfume, it sells for very high prices.

Baleen Horny strips, with a hair-like fringe, from the mouths of toothless whales. Whales use them to filter food from the sea.

Blubber A whale's outer layer of fat, which protects it from the cold and serves as an energy store. It ranges from a thickness of 7.5 cm, in a fin whale, to 50 cm, in a bowhead.

Commercial whaling Hunting whales in order to sell their products, rather than solely for the use of the hunter.

Harpoon A spear with a barbed head.

Hydrogenation A chemical process in which a liquid, such as whale oil, is made to mix with hydrogen. The oil is then purified and becomes hard. Hydrogenation is used to make soap and margarine.

International Whaling Commission (IWC) An organization set up by whaling nations in 1946 to control hunting in order to 'make possible the orderly development of the whaling industry'.

Inuit The native peoples of Alaska, northern Canada and Greenland, once known as Eskimos.

Mammals Warm-blooded animals that give birth to live young, rather than eggs, feeding them with milk.

Moratorium A temporary ban on something.

Rorqual A family of baleen whales. The word 'rorqual' means 'whale with pleats', and these whales all have pleats of skin running under the throat. They expand like a concertina during feeding.

Scrimshaw Sperm whale teeth or bone carved into decorative knick-knacks by sailors.

Spermaceti A very light wax, found in the head of the sperm whale. It was used to make candles and, more recently, as a lubricant in space rockets.

Umiak An Inuit whaling boat, made from seal and walrus skins wrapped on a frame of driftwood.

Windlass A type of horizontal roller used for raising and lowering a ship's anchor. On whaling ships, a windlass was also used for hauling blubber on board.

FURTHER INFORMATION

BOOKS

Whales, Dolphins and Porpoises by Mark Carwardine (Dorling Kindersley, 1992). A highly illustrated children's reference book.

Whale by Vassili Papastavrou (Dorling Kindersley, 1993). Full of photographs, this book has sections on whaling and whale products.

Indians of the Arctic and Subarctic by Paula Younkin (Benford Books, 1992). A children's book on the Inuit, including their hunting of the bowhead whale.

Wooden Ship by Peter Spectre and David Larkin (Houghton Mifflin Company, 1991). Although this is a book for adults, it is simply written and well-illustrated. One chapter looks at the *Charles W. Morgan* whaling ship.

VIDEOS

The Great Whales (National Geographic/IMC Video)

Encounters with Whales (Creation Entertainments) Humpback whales filmed off the coast of Australia.

Whale Song (Earthtrust) A documentary on the whales and dolphins of the Pacific.

INDEX